Above all YO[U]

HAVE

..A..

GOOD

Umbrella

KENDALL'S

Give best Value at Makers' Prices.

Sunshades, Walking Canes, Ladies' Furs.

Re-Covers equal to new from 1/6.   Bring your Repairs.

26 Granby Street (opposite G.P.O.) and 16 Haymarket,

LEICESTER.

Branches throughout England.

LEICESTER
A Pictorial History

Southgate Street by John Flower

LEICESTER
A Pictorial History

Malcolm Elliott

Phillimore

First edition published by Phillimore, 1983
Second Edition, 1999

Published by
PHILLIMORE & CO. LTD.,
Shopwyke Manor Barn, Chichester, West Sussex

© Malcolm Elliott, 1999

ISBN 1 86077 099 1

Printed and bound in Great Britain by
BIDDLES LTD.
Guildford, Surrey

To fellow members of the Leicester Victorian Society, to past and present students, and to my wife who bears with good grace the disruption my obsession with local history so frequently creates.

List of Illustrations

Frontispiece: South Gate Street by John Flower

Bibliography

Everyone who writes about local history in Leicester must owe a debt to the *Victoria County History* which is still incomparable in its range and depth of information. On the earlier periods I have found the series of Archaeological Papers, edited by Mr. Peter Liddle of the Leicestershire Museums Service, invaluable. I also turn frequently to *Radical Leicester* by Professor Temple-Patterson and to the two volumes of *Leicester Past and Present* by Professor Jack Simmons. Much of my information comes from 19th-century guide books and trade directories and newspapers.

Acknowledgments

The Leicestershire Records Office has furnished most of the illustrations used, namely: the frontispiece, 1-2, 10, 12, 15-18, 20-1, 23-8, 30-1, 37-9, 40-1, 43-5, 51-2, 57-64, 66, 73, 83-4, 86, 88-90, 95-7, 102, 106-14, 118, 120, 122-4, 127-38, 140, 148-50, 154-55, 159-63, 166-7. The maps and adverts used as end papers also come from the same collection.

John Lucas of the City Museums Service provided the archaeological material, numbers 3-9, 11, 14 and numbers 13-15, 22, 29, 32-4, 42, 46-7, 53, 55, 67, 69, 156-8 also come from the City Museums Service, mainly through the kind co-operation of Mrs. Yolanda Courtney.

The Leicestershire Archaeological and Historical Society allowed me to photograph material in their library, numbers 46-50, 54, 56, 65, 68, 70, 82, 85, 91-2, 103, 98-100, 126-7, 164-5 for which I thank especially Mr. Aubrey Stevenson.

I am indebted to C.E. John Aston for the use of his collection, numbers 35-6, 80-1, 115-17, 119, 139, 141-44; to Mr. Colin Walker for permission to use the photograph in his 'Main Line Lament'; to Mr. Dennis Callow for numbers 105, 145, 151-2 and to Mrs. Wendy Fraser, a descendant of William Biggs, for the use of 74-6.

The remaining photographs: 19, 71-2, 77-9, 87, 93, 104, 121, 125, 146-7, 153, 168 are my own.

Preface

It has been said that history is a dialogue between past and present, that we engage in conversation with past generations, steering the topics to those which interest us rather than just amassing information about the past for its own sake. Consequently most of us are less interested in history on a broad canvas, such as national or world history, than in the past around us, the story of our own town, village or hamlet; the fastest growing area of historical study today is that of family history.

Interest in tracing one's own ancestors has become a compulsive hobby, as addictive as opium or tobacco and it shows no sign of abating. But the quest for our own forbears is somewhat mechanical and repetitive unless we can relate them to an historical context and invest them with some character. Knowing the sort of clothing they wore, the houses they lived in and the places in which they worked and worshipped enables us to see them as people rather than just names from a census or parish register.

I trust that for Leicester folk, the appearance of a second edition of *Leicester: A Pictorial History* will bring their past to life and help make familiar the world out of which our own has grown.

I want to thank Miss Jean Mellor, formerly the Senior Field Archaeologist with the Leicestershire Museums Service, who gave the benefit of her expertise in advising on the early history of Leicester. I am also grateful to Dr. David Wykes for his comments on the later sections and I would like to thank all those who gave me assistance in particular aspects of the book. I would especially like to thank Mr. John Lucas of the Leicester Museums Service, Mr. Neil Finn of Leicester University Archaeology Service, the staff of the Leicester Record Office and of the City Museums and Art Gallery for all their help so readily given despite the pressures and difficulties they worked under as a result of local government re-organisation.

I wish acknowledge a long-standing debt to Dr. Paul Sternberg, a former student in Leicester and now a professor of ophthalmology at Atlanta, Georgia, U.S.A., for sharing his knowledge of the sanitary history of Leicester and the development of the Victorian water supply. Finally, John Aston, Cynthia Brown, Richard Gill, Roy Millward, Derek Seaton and many other fellow-toilers in the vineyard of local history have helped and guided me in various ways and I extend my warmest thanks to all of them.

M.J.E.

Introduction

Before the Roman Invasion

The earliest evidence of settlement on the site which was to become the city of Leicester dates from about two thousand years ago, in the later Iron Age. Before then the only traces of human activity in the area are the stone tools lost or abandoned by nomadic groups of hunter-gatherers as they moved through the landscape. Some of these stone tools from Leicester date back to the Palaeolithic (Old Stone) Age up to 300,000 years ago, when both the topography and the climate were very different from today.

Even 9,000 years ago the area would be almost unrecognisable. Environmental evidence from a peat deposit filling an ancient water course near the present River Soar indicates an open treeless landscape with marshy areas and stagnant water, perhaps an open pool or ox-bow lake cut off from the main river. The climate too was much colder, similar to that in modern Scandinavia. By about 6,000 years ago it was much more like that of the present day, perhaps even slightly warmer, and much of the area was covered with dense oak forest.

By this time, farming was beginning to be practised in Britain, and this necessitated the clearing of the forest and led to a more settled way of life. Stone axes and other flint tools dating from the Neolithic (New Stone) Age have been found in Leicester, suggesting that here too the forest was being cleared and used for farming and settlement, though no traces of the actual settlements of this period have yet been found.

The relative paucity of pre-Roman burial mounds and other remains should not be taken as evidence of the absence of settlement in this early period. Archaeologists are finding more and more evidence of the dense population of the midland counties during the Stone and Bronze Ages, but the greater productivity of these areas relative to the southern counties during the middle ages destroyed most of the evidence above ground level. As often happened, prosperity in succeeding ages destroyed the traces of earlier habitation.

By the Bronze Age, about 4,000 years ago, there is more definite evidence of settlement in the vicinity of modern Leicester in the form of a cremation urn found below the Royal Arcade, near the High Street, indicating a probable cemetery and settlement nearby. Metalwork and large quantities of Bronze-Age pottery have also been found at Glenfield, which suggests a large settlement here on top of a ridge. Was this perhaps the nucleus of Bronze-Age Leicester?

During the Iron Age, from about 700 B.C., the most familiar type of settlement was the hill-fort, such as Breedon-on-the-Hill, Burrough Hill and Beacon Hill. More common, however, were the small farmsteads for one or two families, like those excavated at Enderby prior to the development of Fosse Park. From around 50 B.C. a similar

1 John Flower's print of the Jewry Wall in the early 19th century when it appears to have been joined at both ends by domestic buildings. The wall formed part of the Roman basilica or complex of government buildings. To the left of the picture is the church of St Nicholas which incorporates material from the Roman basilica.

settlement developed along the east bank of the River Soar and this can be seen as the origin of modern Leicester. From then on the site of the town seems to have been continuously occupied.

In the hundred years or so before the Roman Conquest Leicester seems to have become an important centre for the tribe of the Corieltauvi, which occupied the area of the east Midlands at this time. Although its economic basis was still agricultural, people had trading contacts with south-east Britain and beyond, shown by the presence of pottery manufactured in France, Italy and southern Spain. Fragments of the clay crucibles used in the manufacture of clay coins have also been found, and their presence together with wide trading contacts shows that the settlement, though small in comparison with medieval and Roman Leicester, was already a major regional or tribal centre.

The Roman Period

With the coming of the Romans the evidence becomes much more prolific. After the Claudian invasion of A.D. 43, the legions advanced northwards and may have crossed the Soar somewhere near the present West Bridge. This would have been a convenient fording place for the Fosse Way, that great Roman road that slices through the

2 The Jewry Wall and St Nicholas' Church with the ruins of the Roman bath site in the foreground, before the construction of Vaughan College. The name could refer to a Jewish quarter of the medieval town but there is no evidence to support this and it seems probable that it is a corruption of 'jurats', or councillors, who met in the vicinity.

countryside from Lincoln to the south coast, and which even today provides a direct and relatively peaceful route from Leicester northwards through Newark and south to the Roman town of Corinium or Cirencester.

The grid-like pattern of the town streets seems to have been laid out in the early second century, and increasing Romanisation can be seen in the provision of public buildings such as the forum and basilica and public baths at Jewry Wall, and in the substantial town houses which were provided with features of comfort and sophistication such as tessellated floors, mosaic pavements, central heating and painted wall-plaster. The mosaic from the Blackfriars and the Peacock pavement from St Nicholas Street, now in the Jewry Wall museum, are among the finest in the country.

At some point Ratae Corieltauvorum, as it was then called, was designated the civitas (or tribal capital), the seat of local government and administration for the area. During the later second and early third centuries the town was provided with defences, consisting eventually of an earthen bank, stone wall and ditch, with four main gates and probably several interval towers.

As an important regional centre Ratae was made to reproduce the kind of luxury living to which the Romans were accustomed and a necessary part of civilised

3 The most important of more than two dozen mosaics unearthed in Leicester is the Blackfriars Pavement, found in Jewry Wall Street in 1830. Dating from soon after A.D. 150, it is especially interesting for the way in which the foliage weaves over itself in a naturalistic fashion. When the Great Central Railway cut through Leicester in 1898, special provision was made by Parliament for the preservation of the pavement and for public access to it. Then, with the closure of the railway, the pavement was in danger of destruction from seepage of salts and the decision was taken to remove it to the nearby Jewry Wall museum. This view shows it as it was under the Great Central.

life was the bath house; not just a place in which to wash or swim, but somewhere to meet friends, play at dice, and relax in the hands of a masseur. By a curious coincidence the existence of the baths was not discovered till 1936 when the City Council proposed to build a modern swimming bath on the very same site.

It had long been suspected that the area contained significant Roman remains since it adjoined the Roman Jewry Wall, and so, before commencing building operations, the City Council agreed to a preliminary archaeological survey. The extent of the remains then prompted a full-scale excavation and it became necessary to decide between preserving them or going ahead with the proposed swimming bath. Fortunately, preservation won the day and in 1966 a museum, of material from

4 The Cyparissus Pavement, found as early as 1675 near All Saints' Church. Cyparissus apparently killed his pet stag while hunting and was so upset that the gods took pity on him by turning him into a cypress tree, the symbol of mourning.

prehistoric times down to 1485, was opened to the west of the site, so that visitors may study the actual layout of the baths together with the excellent collection of Roman material in the Jewry Wall museum.

Evidence for the latter part of the Roman period in Leicester is much more fragmentary but it is clear that the town continued to function into the fourth century. Even after the collapse of the Roman Empire, occupation in some form continued, though once again the evidence is mainly limited to finds of Saxon pottery and other objects, while a Saxon cemetery at Thurmaston testifies to a large settlement nearby.

5 The Peacock pavement was found in 1898 in St Nicholas Street, where the *Holiday Inn* now stands. Much of it, including part of the magnificent peacock in the central panel, is a modern reconstruction; the original Roman mosaic is distinguishable by its stippled appearance. The peacock's eye feathers were made with fragments of blue glass. It is dated from the sherds of samian ware used as tesserae soon after A.D. 155.

With the decay of Roman civilisation houses were allowed to fall into ruin, the quarry of later builders, and the regular grid-iron pattern of streets was overlain and submerged with debris and rotting vegetable matter so that the medieval street level is several feet above that of Roman times. The difference in ground level must strike anyone who compares the Jewry Wall baths site with that of the neighbouring church of St Nicholas which was almost certainly built with rubble from the forum and baths.

Saxons and Danes

Many of the buildings of the Roman town probably continued to stand in some form well into the Middle Ages but the clearest indication of Saxon occupation comes from a site, excavated in 1994, on Bonners Lane just outside the Roman south gate, where part of a typical Saxon homestead was revealed.

The recognised centre of the medieval town was its High Cross, at the foot of which food, clothing and other goods were traded from Saxon times, for although there is little archaeological evidence to support the contention, it is likely that Leicester was an established market centre as well as a place of religious importance. By the late seventh century it was important enough to become the seat of a new bishopric, probably located in the church of St Nicholas. Its ecclesiastical eminence from A.D. 679 to 697 was relatively short-lived, however, after which it returned to the see of Lichfield for 40 years. Then in 737 Leicester was re-established as the seat of the diocese and it remained so until the Danish conquest of A.D. 877 caused the amalgamation of the see with that of Lindsey at Dorchester-on-Thames.

It is from this period of its history that the first references to Leicester in anything like its modern form occur, one of the bishops being described in 803 as 'Legorensis civitas episcopus'. Quite what this means is still a matter of doubt, although Professor Ekwall was prepared to accept 'Legra' as an early name of the River Soar akin to the French Loire.

In the late ninth century England suffered the full thrust of Viking invasion, and after 12 years of resistance the great Anglo-Saxon kingdom of Mercia was defeated and partitioned in 877. From this time Leicester became one of the five boroughs of the Danelaw, the military and administrative centre of one of the Danish armies of occupation. Then in 918 Aethelfloeda, daughter of King Alfred of Wessex, succeeded in re-taking the area, and the Danish military dependencies became the basis of the newly-created shires of Leicester, Derby, Nottingham and Lincoln, into which Stamford, the fifth borough, was incorporated.

The Viking threat was not removed, however, and while for the next hundred years the main onslaught came from the Norwegians, it was the Danish King Cnut who emerged triumphant in the early 11th century as ruler of all England and, incidentally, of most of northern Europe as well.

Evidence of the Danish intrusion into the county abounds in the many place-names ending in -by and -thorpe, the latter being daughter settlements of nearby villages, e.g. Barkby and Barkby Thorpe. In the town itself we have several thorough-fares with the word 'gate' appended. This does not generally refer to the entrances to the town, but signifies the way to somewhere, e.g. Belgrave Gate and Humberstone Gate, while the way leading to the gallows was Gallowtree Gate. St Margaret's church may well have been regarded by the Danish community as its own particular place of worship once Christianity had been accepted by the Danes, for both Church Gate and Sanvey Gate (from *sancta via*, the sacred way) lend support to the view that a Danish settlement existed to the north and east of the town alongside that of the Saxons.

The Norman Conquest

Essentially the Norman Conquest of 1066 was but the last of a succession of invasions from Scandinavia, for Normandy itself had only been wrested by Norsemen from the Frankish Kingdom in the tenth century. William's impact proved more lasting, however, than that of his predecessors. He was determined to make good his tenuous claim to the English throne and he established his hold over northern England by a bloody and ruthless campaign of terror. So far as we can tell, Leicester escaped any such carnage.

The valuations of land given in the Domesday Survey of 1086 show little change in the 20 years since the Conquest, which suggests a degree of continuity in the local economy. For the common people life would have carried on much the same, tilling the fields and following their trades as butchers, bakers, fullers and weavers. It did so, however, under the visible shadow of the new overlords, for William erected his great castle mound with its wooden tower and outer bailey as early as 1086, subsequently handing it over to his henchman, Hugh de Grandmesnil.

In the Domesday record, Hugh is listed as the owner of 190 houses in the borough, compared with 39 belonging to the king, out of a total of 322. The population probably numbered about two thousand and there were six churches. Hugh was apparently not satisfied and rose in rebellion two years later, but apparently he survived and was succeeded by his son Ivo, whose death, while on a crusade, brought Leicester into the hands of the de Beaumont earls. It was Robert de Beaumont who established a college close to the castle in 1107, and his son, Robert le Bossu (hunchback), who in 1143 founded the abbey of St Mary de Pratis, beyond the northern wall of the town on the banks of the River Soar. The abbots of Leicester thereafter presented something of a rival power to the temporal presence of the resident earls.

Medieval Magnates: de Montfort and Hastings

To the common people it probably mattered little whether their feudal lord was an abbot or an earl, nor, indeed, whether the earl was a Beaumont or a de Montfort. The de Montforts came onto the scene in 1203, and disappeared with the death of Simon at the Battle of Evesham in 1265. It is sometimes said that Simon, the 'father of English parliaments', showed his generosity to the citizens of Leicester by granting them possession of land, including Victoria Park, but for this there is no foundation whatever, although he did sell some land to the town in the vicinity of what is now Filbert Street. His magnanimity is scarred by his anti-Semitism, however, for in 1231 he granted the burgesses the right to banish all Jews from the town 'until the end of the world', thus giving Leicester the doubtful distinction of ejecting the Jews about sixty years before Edward I made it national policy.

After the Battle of Evesham, Simon's land passed to the Crown and became part of the Duchy of Lancaster, and Leicester became one of the residences of its Lancastrian earls. An enduring monument to their rule is the Trinity Hospital, founded in 1331 for 50 poor and sick people. It remains in existence to this day, providing pleasant and low-cost accommodation for elderly citizens, though the hospital itself now houses the Vice-Chancellor of De Montfort University and the pensioners have obligingly moved to the other side of the river.

In the last 40 years of the 14th century the town probably reached the zenith of its political importance as the favourite residence of John of Gaunt. He entertained both his father, Edward III, and his nephew, Richard II, in his castle. When Gaunt's son came to the throne in 1399 as Henry IV, the town became part of the royal estates and in consequence lost the regular presence of its lord. This must have reduced its prosperity and contributed to the general economic decline of the 15th century, manifested in the decay of several churches and the contraction of the inhabited area of the town. This decline was probably exacerbated by frequent outbreaks of plague.

The chief political influence in the town came to be that of the Hastings family. William, Lord Hastings, the right-hand man of Edward IV, fell an early victim to the ambitions of Richard III. His execution in 1483 led to the cessation of work on his castle at Kirby Muxloe which became a sort of ready-made ruin, testifying to the fall of its mighty founder. But two years later, the fortunes of his family rapidly advanced after the victory of Henry Tudor on the field of Bosworth.

William Wyggeston

It was about the same time that another, humbler but nevertheless wealthy and benevolent, family rose to prominence in Leicester itself. William Wyggeston was a merchant who collected wool from the surrounding countryside and exported it through the Staple at Calais where he was four times mayor. The Staple was the main sales-point for English wool. By forcing all merchants to sell through the one place, English kings were able more easily to exact money from them. The wool-tax was the single most important source of royal revenue. William Wyggeston was also mayor of Leicester twice and M.P. for the borough in 1504. Although twice married, he had no children and left much of his wealth to charity. During his lifetime he endowed a chantry house in the Newarke, and in the following year, 1513, he set about founding a hospital for 12 poor men and, later, 12 poor women of the town. The hospital, which still bears his name, stood on the playground of what is now the Leicester Grammar School. It was not till some years later, however, that the Free Grammar School made its appearance.

In view of the turmoil that characterised these times it is a wonder that the hospital as a religious foundation survived at all. In fact it was strengthened and reformed by Henry Hastings, the third Earl of Huntingdon, in 1576. He was a devout Puritan and saw to it that the newly-appointed master was a man of the same persuasion. The original school had been housed in the disused church of St Peter, but in 1573 this was demolished to provide building stone for the new school, which still stands on the corner of Freeschool Lane and High Cross Street.

While the people of Leicester had cause to remember the Wyggestons with gratitude as founders of the hospital and Free Grammar School, the family is remembered today almost as much for the beautiful house owned by Roger Wyggeston in High Cross Street, now used to house the Costume Museum. They also live on in the visual record of domestic piety recorded on the glass panels from this house, a priceless and unique record of medieval life now displayed in the Jewry Wall museum.

William Wyggeston's piety reflects the religious fervour of his time. He lived through the entire period of the king's divorce, and the deaths of Wolsey in Leicester Abbey and

6 Public interest in archaeological digs has grown in recent years. Here a local archaeologist, Mr. Terry Pearce, explains the significance of trenches on the site at Great Holme Street revealed when Victorian terraces like that shown here were demolished in the 1970s.

of More on the scaffold. He died in 1536, the same year as the suppression of the minor religious houses and the Pilgrimage of Grace. Political life was equally eventful. Born in the middle of what were later to be known as 'the Wars of the Roses', Wyggeston doubtless heard talk of the marriage of the beautiful Elizabeth Woodville, widow of Sir John Grey of Groby, to the handsome King Edward IV. He would have known of the death of Lord Hastings of Kirby, and must surely have seen King Richard go riding out of Leicester to his defeat at Bosworth Field in August 1485. He may well also have witnessed his ignominious return, slung naked over a horse to be exposed to the public gaze for two days before being buried in the church of the Grey Friars.

Religious and secular history combined in the fall of Wolsey and his death in Leicester Abbey in 1529. Within ten years the abbey itself was to be destroyed as part of that great ferment known as the Reformation. Whatever the religious or political arguments in favour of the break with Rome, one can only regret the wholesale destruction of art and architecture that accompanied the dissolution of the monasteries. It was first proposed to make Leicester Abbey into a cathedral, which might yet have soared majestically into the sky like Peterborough or Lincoln, but alas it was plundered and reduced to rubble and the stark lines delineating its site today date only from the 1930s.

Lady Jane Grey of Bradgate

Elizabeth Woodville was not the only member of the Grey family with a taste for grand marriages. Henry Grey, whose father had built the great house in Bradgate Park, married the daughter of the Duke of Suffolk—a niece of Henry VIII. Thus his own daughter, Jane, had strong claims to the throne, if Mary and Elizabeth were excluded. Jane herself had no wish to be a pawn in the political machinations of her father-in-law. 'The crown is not my right', she protested, 'the Lady Mary is the rightful Queen.' Nevertheless, she suffered the ultimate penalty for the ambitions of others reigning for nine days before her confinement and eventual execution in the Tower.

Local patriotism doubtless brought more than usual sympathy for Lady Jane in Leicester, but the town was wise enough to declare its allegiance to Mary in 1554. By contrast with the Hastings family, the Greys never seem to have concerned themselves much with the affairs of the town and, at some time in the early 18th century, they ceased even to visit Bradgate. Ownership of the park remained with the Grey family, however, until 1928 when it was bought in a splendid gesture of public beneficence by Charles Bennion, founder of the British United Shoe Machinery Company, and given to the people of Leicestershire.

Rivalry between the Greys and the Hastings inevitably showed itself in the tempestuous years of the Civil War in the 17th century. The Greys sided with parliament, while the Earl of Huntingdon and Colonel Hastings stood for the king. The unfortunate townsfolk were first wooed and then bullied by each in turn. Acting with ruthless zeal, Prince Rupert demanded £2,000 from Leicester at the outbreak of the war in September 1642. Charles's disavowal of this demand did little to mollify the town or to win him the confidence of his nephew. For the next three years Leicester was held for parliament by Lord Grey, but on 30 May 1645 Rupert began a siege and bombardment that ended in the capitulation and sack of the town. One hundred and forty cartloads of gold and silver and other valuables were removed from Leicester, including the Corporation mace and insignia.

The king's victory was to be his last. A fortnight later the fate of Charles and his army was sealed at the battle of Naseby just over the southern border of the county. How far ordinary people suffered as a consequence of the Civil War is difficult to say. It was to the advantage of each side to exaggerate the barbarity of the other, so that accounts of wholesale massacre by the king's troops are generally discounted, but there must have been considerable hardship following Rupert's siege. Moreover the actions of Sir Thomas Fairfax in regaining the town for parliament brought more suffering to the poor. A petition of the mayor and aldermen stated that 'above one Hundred and Twenty dwelling howses of poore men have beene pulled downe and much ground

7 Excavations in Norfolk Street, west of the River Soar and close to the junction of Hinckley Road and Fosse Road Central, revealed evidence of an extensive Roman villa of the late second century A.D. This is an artist's impression of how it probably looked.

digged up and spoyled in and about the said workes'. The destitute inhabitants were thrown onto parish relief:

> The burthen whereof growes so great that your peticioners are not able to beare the same beinge extraordinarily plundred and wasted by the king's forces at the takinge of this Town and many poor widdowes whose husbands were slayne at the same tyme and they thereby disabled to subsist and mayntayne themselves and their poor famylies are very chardgable to your peticioners to provide for and keepe.

The Growth of Religious Dissent

The Civil War had a mixture of origins: political, economic and social, though religious differences were paramount and, as always in time of war, men fortified their actions with the passionate belief that God was exclusively on their side. King Charles appealed to an instinctive conservatism, to episcopacy and the prayer-book and an immemorial order of society in which all men knew their place and in which God had ordained him as king. The forces opposed to him sprang from a more complex ideological soil, ranging from political opponents to Puritans who rejected all outward authority but that of their own interpretation of the Bible.

It was perhaps natural that Leicestershire with its Lollard traditions should produce some fervent champions of religious freedom and it did. George Fox, the founder of Quakerism, was born in Fenny Drayton in 1624. As a young man at the outset of the Civil War he was engrossed in his own personal quest for religious truth, finding it ultimately in the 'inward light of Christ' which he claimed was in every man and woman. It was this insistence on the equality of the sexes that led to his first brush with authority, when he argued the right of a woman to speak in St Martin's Church. By 1699 Fox had about 40,000 followers in the country at large and there were over a dozen Quaker meeting houses in Leicestershire. After the 1689 Toleration Act and the ending of persecution, the ardour of early Quakers turned inward, while their diligence and simple lifestyle led many of them to prosper in industry and commerce.

John Bunyan vigorously denounced Fox and his followers and his more orthodox Calvinism took a firm hold in Leicestershire, the Baptists becoming the most numerous of the nonconformist churches. Their numerical strength does not seem to have been noteworthy until the late 18th century, however, and enthusiasm for the Baptists may well reflect the general rekindling of religious fervour associated with John Wesley in the mid-century. Methodism made its greatest impact on the poor and the industrial artisans. Its apparent lack of interest in the souls of the wealthy led Selina, Countess of Huntingdon, to establish her own brand of evangelism in 1781, known as 'The Countess of Huntingdon's Connexion'. Through this means she devoted her considerable wealth and talents to educating a body of young preachers whose vocation was to preach the gospel to the affluent classes.

For the most part the citizens of Leicester were untroubled by the varieties of religious experience. The devotion of its mayor and corporation to High Anglicanism brought them perilously close to supporting Charles Stuart in the rebellion of '45. They were saved from such a course only by the decision of Prince Charles to turn back at the Leicestershire border and return to Scotland. During the late 18th century the rigid devotion of Leicester Corporation to Anglican Toryism made it increasingly obnoxious to the growing number of prosperous families who made up the congregation of the Presbyterian chapel in East Bond Street. By the early 19th century the great Meeting had become Unitarian and the focus of opposition to the political and religious monopoly of the Old Corporation.

Economic Developments

In the late 17th century a new industry was taking root in Leicestershire as hosiers came to organise the manufacture of stockings by hand. The stocking-frame was introduced in the 1690s in response to increased demand, supplementing traditional production by hand. By the mid-18th century frame-knitted stockings dominated the market and hosiers found it more profitable to install frames in the East Midlands than in the London area, where the Company of Framework Knitters exercised greater control over pay and conditions. Thus cheap labour, together with the availability of wool, was a primary cause of Leicester's rising prosperity as a hosiery town.

The stocking-frame had been invented by William Lee in 1589, pre-dating by 200 years the technical inventions in production of cloth that sparked off the Industrial Revolution. Yet, having been so far ahead of the field among the various branches of the textile trade, the knitting of hosiery remained stubbornly resistant to the use of anything but hand power in its operation. It was not till the mid-19th century that a workable steam-powered circular knitting-machine transformed the cottage industry into a factory one. The making of worsted yarn, however, could well have been done by steam power, using a variant of Arkwright's water-frame, had it not been for the determination of local men to resist the threat to their jobs. In 1787 the firm of Coltman and Whetstone attempted to introduce such a machine but this resulted in a week-long riot in Northgate Street during which Whetstone was lucky to escape with his life. There can be no doubt that the refusal of the authorities to intervene was due in part to the religious and political views of the hosiers.

The Reformed Corporation of 1836

On the broader national front, High Toryism suffered a resounding blow in the wake of the Great Reform Bill of 1832. The new Whig administration turned its attention to a variety of matters ripe for reform including the government of corporate towns. The commissioners sent to enquire into the workings of municipal corporations found ample argument for radical reform in the bribery, corruption and general inertia of the old system in Leicester. Not surprisingly the Old Corporation and its chief servant, Thomas Burbidge, the Town Clerk, fought desperately to resist any changes but the new ratepayer franchise swept them from power in Leicester until well into the next century. When the new Corporation met for the first time on 31 December 1835 only four out of 42 were Conservatives and, of those, two were only chosen by the casting vote of the retiring mayor.

Change was in the air. The transformation of England from a rural economy to a predominantly urban one had already begun in the late 18th century. Although some individuals in the county had been prominent among the pioneers of agricultural and industrial change, Leicester remained largely untouched by the coming of power machinery until well into the 19th century. That is not to say it remained unchanged, however, for the lure of the town to unemployed rural labourers and to Irish immigrants brought a steady rise in population and the growth of squalid courts of cheap housing, filling up the gardens and orchards of the town and spilling into the neighbouring fields.

Canals and Railways

Change came too in links with the rest of the country. The old system of roads radiating from the town had been improved in the 18th century by the operation of Turnpike Trusts which raised tolls for highway maintenance. Then, in 1794, the canal reached Leicester from Loughborough, bringing coal from the Nottingham and Derby coalfield via the Erewash canal across the River Trent. It took another 20 years for the through route to London, via Foxton locks, to be completed, but improved transportation lowered costs, especially that of fuel. In 1820, 115 tons of coal was carried to Leicester, roughly half for distribution elsewhere, compared with only 11½ tons for all other merchandise.

It was this heavy traffic in coal which brought the railway from Swannington in 1832, the earliest in the Midlands. Leicestershire coal owners were keen to regain their traditional market and the prospect of a novel and cheap means of bringing their supplies to the Leicester market was immediately attractive. Prime movers in the enterprise were William Stenson of Whitwick, Joseph Whetstone, whose grandfather survived the riots of 1787, and Samuel Smith Harris, the future borough surveyor, the latter both members of the Unitarian Great Meeting congregation, and John Ellis, a Quaker farmer of Beaumont Leys. Ellis was introduced to George Stephenson through his Quaker friends in Stockton and Darlington and thus procured the services of Robert Stephenson as engineer to the local line. The Leicester-Swannington, which opened in 1832, incorporated several unique features: the Glenfield railway tunnel, the longest in existence at the time, the lift-bridge designed to take coal trucks over the canal to the Leicester goods yard of Ellis and Everard, and the stationary engine, now in York Railway Museum, that pulled coal to the top of Swannington incline.

The Leicester-Swannington line merged with the Midland Railway in 1847 and John Ellis, now residing at Belgrave Hall, became its Chairman. The Swannington line finally closed in 1965 and the tunnel ends were bricked up to prevent mischief or accidents. The ventilation shafts alone remain to mark the course of one of the earliest railways in the world and they have now been added to the official list of buildings of historic interest at the Department of the Environment.

Economic and Social Development of the Victorian Town

The new Corporation was hampered by a legal dispute with the former Town Clerk, Thomas Burbidge, who, though suspected of dipping his fingers into the public purse, had the effrontery to demand compensation for loss of office under the terms of the Municipal Corporations Act of 1835. Consequently the range of activity undertaken by the new town government was limited by the desire to save money. One innovation laid on the Council by the Act was the establishment of a new and efficient police force. Frederick Goodyer was appointed superintendent in February 1836,

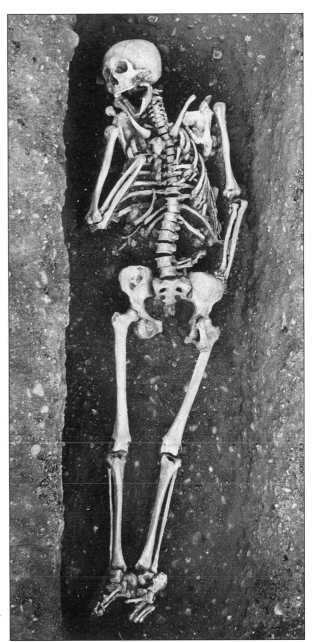

8 Skeleton of a Roman lady excavated in 1975 from the Norfolk Street site. This lies to the west of the River Soar, close to the junction of Fosse Road and King Richard's Road. The Victorians came across tesselated pavements here in the course of grubbing out an old cherry orchard. More recent and careful excavation revealed continuous occupation of the site from the Iron Age through to late Roman times. The lady shown here was evidently buried with her boots on.

bringing with him the discipline and training he had acquired while serving with the Metropolitan Police Force. The new police force was at first feared, especially by local Conservatives, as a foretaste of continental despotism, but it rapidly proved its worth in the maintenance of law and order and in the reduction of petty crime. Moreover, when the council turned its attention to other matters, such as the removal of public nuisances, it utilised the services of the constabulary and appointed Goodyer as its Inspector of Nuisances.

Goodyer relinquished his posts with the borough in 1839 in order to take up a more lucrative position as head of the new county constabulary, and it was Goodyer's successor as Inspector of Nuisances, the aged radical, George Bown, who suggested the appointment of the first medical officers appointed by any local authority in Britain. They took up their duties in October 1846 and became prime movers in the promotion of public health measures such as the need for a comprehensive system of sewerage and water supply.

Leicester was among the first towns to establish a municipal water supply, drawn from a reservoir at Thornton, some eight miles to the west. By a fitting coincidence, the first place to receive these pure waters was the Temperance Hall in Granby Street in December 1853. The Temperance Movement in Leicester owed much of its success to the flair and acumen of Thomas Cook, the travel agent. His first venture into the package tour business began in July 1841 when he hired a train to take a party of temperance advocates from Leicester to Loughborough Park. Ten years later, he was instrumental in organising the visits of tens of thousands to the Great Exhibition at the Crystal Palace in London.

Progress in hosiery manufacture, the town's principal industry, was hampered until the coming of power machinery in the 1860s. In this respect Leicester seems to have lagged behind its northern neighbour, Loughborough, where William Cotton's enterprise and skill had created a machine-powered industry a decade earlier. In Leicester, the crucial innovation seems to have come first via some of the machines of Hine and Mundella of Nottingham which were installed at the St Margaret's works of Thomas Corah in 1865. Mundella was a native of Leicester who built up a thriving business in Nottingham and became a prominent M.P. for Sheffield. It was probably the competitive edge gained by Corah's that sealed the fate of the great hosiery business of John Biggs. At one time the Biggs brothers employed 12,000 people. They were members of the Unitarian Great Meeting and both John and William were thrice mayor of Leicester and Members of Parliament. John took a leading part in the affairs of the town, promoting his own radical newspaper, The *Leicestershire Mercury*, which advocated civic improvement such as the demolition of the old town hall and the erection of a new one. It seems entirely fitting that this vigorous and ebullient man should be one of the few to be commemorated on a statue in the city, in Welford Place, where he stands appropriately close to the hub of present-day civic government in the New Walk Centre.

John Biggs did not live to see the opening of the new Town Hall in 1872 nor the removal of the cattle market from the centre to the edge of the town on Aylestone Road. Fortunately for us, the old town hall was not demolished but neither was it replaced, for the new municipal buildings deliberately excluded any grand hall or meeting rooms as these were well supplied by the Opera House and the Temperance Hall. It was not till 1913 therefore that the town was eventually provided with the De Montfort Hall, a civic hall capable of holding large numbers of people.

The great improvement in Leicester's economic prosperity came with the expansion of its industrial base to include shoe manufacture and light engineering from the mid-19th century. This was reflected in a 40 per cent rise in its population in the decade after 1861. In 1842 the desperate poverty of its stocking knitters had made Leicester a leading centre of Chartist activity, but when the firebrand leader of Leicester's working men looked back from the perspective of 1872, he commented: 'How different is the condition of Leicester now thirty years have gone! All who enter it for the first time are pleased with the air of thrift the town wears, and the moving population of the streets. I saw lounging groups of men in my time.'

By the late 19th century shoe machinery, lift manufacture, the making of cycles, typewriters, umbrellas and sewing-machines had been added to the town's chief industries. Businesses often expanded or grew out of others; for instance, much of the town's engineering sprang originally from making hosiery frames. Joseph Goddard's silver-plate powder was produced in his chemist's shop as an alternative to abrasive polishes on silver-plated surfaces. By the end of the century his business was able to lend capital to help found other firms such as Wadkins, Imperial Typewriters and the Bentley Engineering Company.

The Changing Face of Leicester

It is to the decades of vigorous industrial expansion that we owe the predominant architecture of modern Leicester. Most of the town's medieval heritage, so lovingly depicted by John Flower, was demolished in the mid-19th century to be replaced by brick-built tenements and factories. Even the elegant stucco fronts of 18th and early 19th-century buildings were viewed with scorn by the Victorians and replaced by what they saw as more honest and robust brick structures. There was a passion for gabled roofs and bay windows, while decorative detail flowered on every conceivable elevation.

It was in part the Victorian passion for cleanliness and order that sealed the fate of John Flower's mud-and-wattle townscape. Half-timbered houses and primitive street drains probably helped to give Leicester that eminence in the rates of mortality which rightly appalled 19th-century reformers. When we look at the paintings of Fulleylove, Henton and Mary Sloane we share their feeling for red brick rather than wood and plaster, for the legacy that absorbed Flower had already passed away.

Nineteenth-century improvers had few qualms about reducing old buildings to rubble as the central core of towns like Leicester spawned bigger and bigger offices, shops and factories. The needs of urban traffic also accounted for much destruction, especially on account of railway development but also as horse-drawn vehicles multiplied on the old carriageways. Road-widening led to the destruction of the *Blue Boar* inn and St Ursula's Chapel while, at the start of the twentieth century, the Huntingdon Tower was sacrificed to the path of the electric tram.

Rising living standards and government subsidies in the 20th century led to the removal of much early Victorian working-class housing and to the creation of model housing estates on the outskirts of the town. Such social engineering brought its own

9 A Roman actor's mask. This is a detail from the Roman wall painting found during excavation of a town house in Blue Boar Lane in the 1950s. The murals are about ten feet high and show draped figures set against architectural perspectives.

problems, however, and by the late 1970s Leicester City Council had adopted a policy of retention and renewal of its housing stock rather than wholesale destruction.

With the diversification of industry prosperity replaced poverty and, in the 1920s, Leicester gained a reputation as the 'richest city of the Empire'. Yet it was in fact largely the buoyancy of the traditional hosiery industry during the First World War that created new wealth and, despite the growth of new industries, textiles, knitwear and clothing remain probably the largest employers of labour in the private sector.

It was partly the opportunities presented in hosiery that attracted large numbers of people from East Africa, fleeing the attrocities of Idi Amin in the early 1970s, that has led to the most striking social characteristic of modern Leicester, that is its cultural diversity. We have a city where racial integration is everywhere apparent and accepted as a fact of life. Leicester is justly proud of its multi-cultural identity.

In the 20th century the motor car has changed the face of our towns and villages, just as the motorways have scarred the rural landscape with an appetite even more voracious than that of the railways. That appetite has to be curbed by sensible control over the location of shopping centres and by the provision of attractive means of public transport in order to sustain the economic life of town centres. Coupled with this is the need to preserve what is best in the architectural heritage bequeathed to us by past generations. Unless we do this our towns will lose their individual character and identity and all our lives will be the poorer.

10 Two workmen dug up this Roman milestone at Thurmaston in 1771. It served as a garden roller for some years and was set up in Belgrave Gate in 1783 as part of the obelisk depicted here by John Flower. The stone is now in the Jewry Wall Museum.

11 Site of a Saxon House on Bonners Lane, unearthed in 1993. To the layman, one hole looks much like another, but the archaeologists were highly excited by this one as its features indicate the first clear evidence of a Saxon settlement close to the edge of the Roman town. The photograph shows a shallow L-shaped feature in the centre of the picture with eight large postholes visible against the internal edges of the cut. The circular brick structure is a 19th-century well, while the V-shaped feature to the right of it is a partially excavated 17th-century ditch, thought to be part of Leicester's Civil War defences. The photo was kindly supplied by Neil Finn of the University of Leicester Archaeological Survey team.

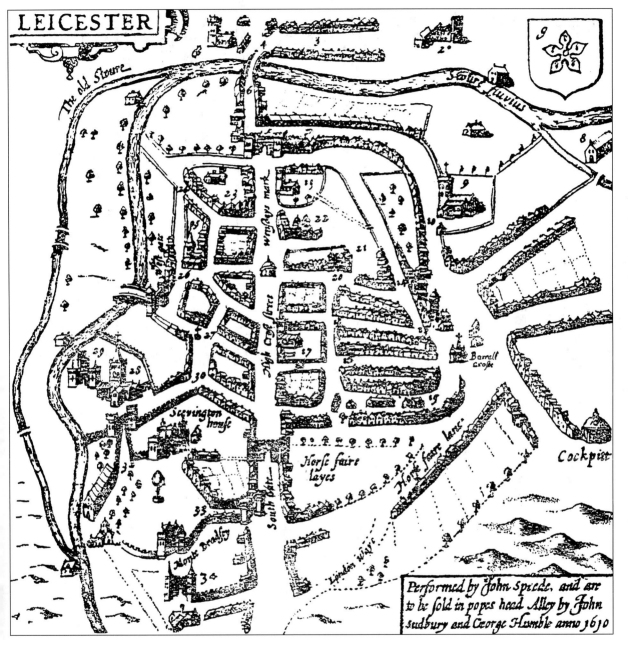

12 Speed's map of 1610. John Speed produced a series of maps covering most of the country and his county maps usually contained inset plans of the chief towns and cities. This is his plan of Leicester together with the explanatory legend.

13 Painted glass panels from the house of Roger Wyggeston, dating from 1495. These are some of the very few pieces of glass to have survived the Reformation and are unique in that they come from a domestic and not a religious house. It is thought they escaped destruction from Puritan zeal through their being enclosed in the fabric of the walls of the house, now the Costume Museum. The glass itself is now in the Jewry Wall museum.

14 Medieval undercroft with Roman floor remains beneath the service yard of the former Antiques Centre on Guildhall Lane and St Nicholas Circle. The picture was taken with a fish-eye lens to show the whole cellar rather than a single wall. The site lies just to the north of the Roman forum.

15 An 18th-century view of the town showing corn growing on the south field and several windmills around the site of Mill Lane. On the extreme right is St Margaret's Church and on the far left is Danet's Hall. This is taken from an engraving by the Buck brothers in 1743.

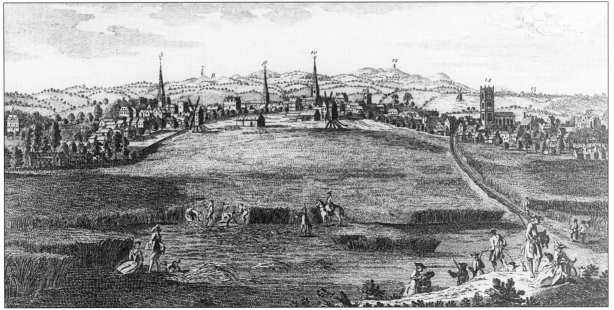

16 St Margaret's Church stood just beyond the walls of the town giving the name to two of its principal thoroughfares: Church Gate and Sanvey Gate, a corruption of Sancta Via, i.e. the sacred way to the church. The name became a household word after its adoption by Corah's for ladies' garments supplied to Marks and Spencer. The corresponding trade mark for men's wear was St Michael's. The spacious grandeur of St Margaret's, with its perpendicular tower, of 1444 makes it the most cathedral-like of all Leicester's churches, though the honour of that title went, of course, to the more centrally-placed St Martin's.

17 John Flower drew this view of the Guildhall in the 1820s when it was still in use as both a prison and the meeting place of the Town Council. The Guildhall dates from the late 14th century and was originally the home of the Guild of Corpus Christi founded in 1343. It was acquired by the Corporation after the dissolution of the Guild in 1547. With the opening of the new Town Hall in 1876, the old Guildhall was left empty for a while and many urged its destruction as a 'rat infested barn'. Fortunately, James Thompson, the founder and editor of the *Leicester Mercury*, pleaded successfully for its retention.

18 St Martin's Church, elevated to cathedral status in 1927, as illustrated in John Nichols (1791), with its original porch, later resurrected as the porch of St Nicholas. It was much restored by several Victorian architects: J.L. Pearson and G.E. Street worked on the aisles and Raphael Brandon gave it the imposing tower and spire of 1862.

19 The timber-framed medieval Merchant's Hall in Silver Street is one of the least-known architectural gems of Leicester. Until recently it was a carpet store and threatened with decay and demolition, but a wise decision by the City Council led to its restoration. It is now Ask's Pizzera.

20 Kirby Muxloe, now within the boundaries of the town, retains its identity as a separate village. William, Lord Hastings began to build his great moated castle of brick, one of the earliest to be so constructed, but his efforts ceased abruptly when he fell victim to the anger of Richard III and was beheaded in October 1483. It has thus always appeared ruinous, as in this print of John Flower's.

21 The Abbey of St Mary in the Meadows was founded by Robert le Bossu in 1143. It became the second richest Augustinian house in England but there is no surviving record of its appearance and, of the 900 books once in its library, only six or seven survive. It was dissolved at the order of Henry VIII in 1539. Nine years earlier, Cardinal Wolsey rested his weary bones in the shelter of the Abbey and fortuitously died, doubtless preferring to meet his maker in the next world rather than his master in this. Archaeologists dug the site in the 1930s and it is on the basis of their findings that these rubble walls were constructed to show where the great church and its cloisters once stood.

22 One of Mary Linwood's needlework pictures showing Cardinal Wolsey arriving at Leicester Abbey and seeking hospitality with the words: 'Father Abbot, I am come to rest my weary bones among you'. He died two days later and was buried in the Abbey church.

23 A view of the Abbey meadows in the mid-19th century before the creation of Abbey Park. The River Soar lapped close to the Abbey walls and meandered over the flat expanse of meadow in what one commentator, fearing the waste of ratepayers' money in the creation of the park, called 'that dank, diphtherial and febrile spot'.

24 After the dissolution of the monasteries, Leicester Abbey, in common with most others, was quickly robbed of its valuable lead, stone and other building materials. Part of the gatehouse survived and was absorbed into a mansion built by the Earl of Huntingdon. Known as Cavendish House, it was burned down during the Civil War. This is how it looked by 1730.

South View.

25 & 26 In the late 19th century market gardens filled the space close to the ruins of Cavendish House.

27 The interior of Leicester Castle as it appeared in the early 19th century, just before its extensive remodelling. The spacious interior was divided into panelled court rooms for the County magistrates and Assize Courts. None of the pillars survives intact, but the base of one and the capital of another do exist as does the far wall with its Anglo-Norman windows. As the residence of the Dukes of Lancaster, the castle had been the administrative hub of their vast estates. John of Gaunt lived here and entertained the young King, Richard II, and it was here that the same king was brought as a prisoner, before his deposition by Gaunt's son, Henry IV. In the words of the historian James Thompson, it was 'more than a baronial mansion—it was the Palace of the Midlands during the most splendid period of the Middle Ages'. After the Duchy was absorbed by the Crown in 1399, Leicester ceased to play such an important role and its castle remained virtually untouched until 1821.

28 John Flower's view of the Newarke Gateway in the mid-19th century. This was the main entrance to the 'new works', or the extension to the bailey of the medieval castle, of the 14th century.

29 South Wall of the Newarke in about 1880, just before it was demolished, from the corner of Fairfax Street.

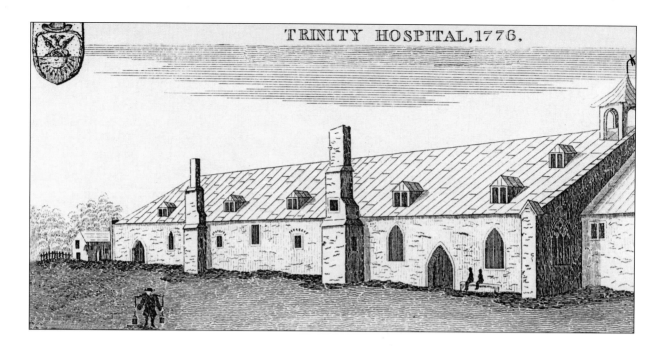

TRINITY HOSPITAL, 1776.

30 Trinity Hospital as illustrated by John Nichols in his great work on the *History of Leicestershire*, first published in 1791. Founded by Henry, Earl of Leicester, in 1331 as a hospital for 50 old men, the foundation still provides pleasant homes for elderly citizens but the building itself is now part of De Montfort University and contains the Vice-Chancellor's office. In the 1796 view, the hospital almost adjoins St Mary's Vicarage, effectively forming an enclosed quadrangle. The opening of the new bridge over the canal in 1898 necessitated the realignment of the hospital and its virtual rebuilding in 1902.

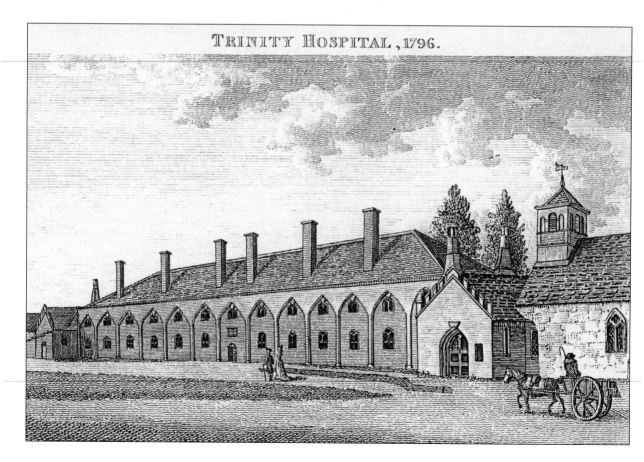

TRINITY HOSPITAL, 1796.

31 An early 19th-century view of the house in the Newarke with the spires of St Mary de Castro on the left and of St Martin's on the right.

32 The Newarke in the late 18th century. St Mary's Vicarage is in the distance and Trinity Hospital to the right. The house in the centre left was built about 1690 on the site of the Church of the Annunciation of Our Lady. It may have been connected with the annual feast of Corpus Christi, when a procession of Virgins, together with 12 men representing the apostles, converged on the Church of St Margaret from various parts of the town.

33   Edward Shipley Ellis, son of John Ellis, the railway pioneer, who himself became chairman of the Midland Railway Company, lived in this house till his death in 1879. The house was demolished to build the Technical College in 1889 which became the core of the De Montfort University.

34   St Mary's Vicarage in the 1920s, at the lower end of the Newarke adjacent to Trinity Hospital. It was probably provided originally for one of the canons of the college of the Newarke which stood on the site of the Hawthorne Building until the Reformation. In the early years of the 20th century it was part of the Wyggeston Girls School. In 1947 the top two storeys were removed, but there are hopes that the present ownership by De Montfort University may lead to its restoration.

35   The Newarke Gateway in 1902, with a flock of sheep being driven down Oxford Street and Southgate Street.

36 St Mary de Castro seen above the Turret Gateway. To the right of the Gateway is an iron works or forge standing on what is now the garden of the Newarke Houses museum.

37 & 38 Arguably the finest medieval building in Leicester was the Chapel of St Ursula at the Wyggeston Hospital, as depicted in John Nichols *History of Leicestershire* in 1791. It was founded in 1513 for 12 poor men and 12 poor women who were to be 'very aged, decrepit, blynde, lame or maymed, or that wantith natural witt'. It stretched from the roadway to the west end of St Martin's Church and was demolished in 1875. One of its porches was moved to the church of St Nicholas and the pulpit to the chapel of Trinity Hospital, but the materials and fittings, including the massive roof timbers and bell turret, were sold off for £92.

39 The Victorian successor to the Wyggeston Hospital, designed by T.C. Sorby, the Crown Surveyor, was erected on the Hinckley Road in 1867, and was itself demolished in the 1960s to be replaced by more convenient accommodation on the same site. The Wyggeston family were by far the wealthiest in Leicester at the beginning of the 16th century, William Wyggeston being a Mayor of the Staple at Calais. Part of his foundation later became the Free School and, by a somewhat tenuous thread, the present Wyggeston schools also claim him as their founder.

40 The Free School, High Cross Street, in 1791. The endowment of William Wyggeston was greatly advanced by the Earl of Huntingdon in the reign of Elizabeth I, but by 1841 the school had ceased to function and pupils were entrusted to other places of education till the setting up of the new Wyggeston School in 1877. This building is currently used by a car rental firm.

41 Henry Hastings, 3rd Earl of Huntingdon, from a portrait by Christopher Carter in the City Museum and Art Gallery. William, Lord Hastings was executed by order of the king in 1483, but, following the defeat of Richard III at Bosworth, the fortunes of his family started to rise. They became Earls of Huntingdon from 1529, the 3rd Earl holding the title from 1559 to 1595. Under him the influence of the Hastings family in the town was at its height; his fervent puritanism endeared him to the townsfolk and he drew up regulations for both the Free Grammar School and Wyggeston's Hospital.

42 A sketch by John Flower of St Mary's Church, Knighton, its 13th-century tower embellished by a statue that survived the Reformation. Oram's cottage is in the foreground and is one of the few medieval cottages still standing within the city boundaries. To the right can be seen the farm buildings which remained close to the church till the 1930s, standing in what is now the graveyard of the church.

43 Bow Bridge, as illustrated in Nichols' History (1791), by which Richard III left Leicester on his way to Bosworth Field. The single-arched bridge in the foreground, known as the Little Robber Bridge, fell down in the same year, 1791, but its shape seems to have given the name to the five-arched bridge that stands behind. This was demolished in 1863 to be replaced by the iron bridge that lasted until the road improvements of the 1970s.

44 The old West Bridge became overloaded and inadequate by the start of Victoria's reign and an Improvement Act was passed in 1841 with the primary purpose of building a new bridge. William Flint's elegant answer to the problem, erected in 1841, was unable to bear the increased traffic of 50 years later and it too was demolished to be replaced by the present bridge, now complemented by a second span to the north.

45 The medieval pack-horse bridge over the Soar at Aylestone, one of several by which produce, including coal from the pits of north-west Leicestershire, was carried across the river to the Leicester market.

46 Aylestone Mill in 1885. There are four mills listed in the Domesday Book entry for Aylestone. This one, sketched by the daughter of John Flower, stood opposite Grace Road. Note the post windmill on the hill behind. Both water- and windmills catered for fields of corn which are now covered with houses.

47 A sketch by John Flower of Aylestone Hall before its restoration in 1850. Behind a rather dull exterior there is an early 15th-century core. The hall belonged to the Vernons of Haddon Hall. About 1563, Dorothy Vernon married John Manners, Duke of Rutland, in the church a short distance away.

48 Braunstone Hall, now a junior school, was designed by William Oldham for Clement Winstanley in 1776. This fine Georgian house has a delightful walled rose garden, ornamental lake and extensive grounds that now form Braunstone Park. The estate was bought by the Corporation in 1929 and laid out as the largest of its inter-war housing estates.

49 Before their rise to wealth and importance on the national stage, the Hastings family had lived at Braunstone. Nothing remains of their manor house but the neighbouring church retains some features, such as the tower, from medieval times. This is the church as illustrated in Nichols.

50 The Huntingdon Tower stood at the junction of High Street and Union Street. It was all that remained of the town residence of the 3rd Earl of Huntingdon who was Lord Lieutenant of Leicestershire from 1559 to 1595. Many notable people lodged here, including Mary Queen of Scots, James I in 1612, Charles I in 1642 and his nephew Prince Rupert. Mary Sloane sketched this view of the Tower shortly before its demolition in 1902.

51 John Flower's view of High Cross Street shows the High Cross in its original position at the junction with High Street. Sellers of eggs and fruit can be seen, as this remained the weekday market until 1883. In the background is the old Free School and the County Gaol. To the left, on a side wall, can be seen election posters of June 1826 reading: 'Evans for Ever', 'Hastings for Free Trade' and 'Cave and a large Loaf', testifying to the perennial importance of free trade and protection as an election issue.

52 The Elizabethan High Cross of Leicester was an octagonal structure rather like the one that still stands in the centre of Mountsorrel. It was replaced by a single one of its pillars in 1769 but even this was found to be an obstruction to traffic and in 1836 it was removed. Red granite setts in the roadway at the junction of High Street and High Cross Street mark the spot where it used to stand.

LEICESTER CROSS.
built 1577; taken down 1769.

53 In the Middle Ages every town had its cross as a place for meeting other people, for buying and selling goods and publishing proclamations. The column we now know in the corner of the Market Place is just part of Leicester's medieval High Cross. This remaining column was removed in 1836 and placed in front of The Crescent, King Street, by James Rawson, the last mayor of the old Corporation. The Crescent, built in 1826 to the design of William Firmadge, was residential accommodation until it was gutted in the 1960s and turned into offices.

54 Arthur Wakerley bought the Crescent in 1915 in order to acquire the Cross as a garden ornament for his house on Gwendolen Road. North Evington was virtually created by Arthur Wakerley and several of the streets bear the names of members of his family: there are Dorothy, Constance and Margaret Roads as well as Gwendolen. In 1952 the High Cross was placed in the garden of the Newarke Houses Museum from where it was removed in 1976 by the Rotary Club to the corner of the Market Place where it stands today. The commemorative plaque on the plinth incorporates a free translation from the infamous Little Red Book of Chairman Mao.

55 George Shirley Harris, a hosier, and his family in the grounds of their home, Skeffington House in the Newarke, 1867.

56 The Chantry House, built in 1512 for two chantry priests supported by William Wyggeston to say services in the Collegiate church. It was saved from destruction by the Leicestershire Archaeological and Historical Society in 1912 and is now part of the Leicester City Newarke Houses Museum.

57 The Castle and St Mary de Castro from across the river. This photograph of about 1890 shows how the river must have looked prior to the engineering works which led to the construction of the New Cut, the mile-long stretch of embankments lining the deepened and canalised river Soar south of the West Bridge. The area in front of the church and castle became castle Gardens in 1929.

58 A water-colour by W. Millican of New Gainsborough or Exchange, built in 1747 to replace the old Gainsborough. The upper rooms were used as the magistrates' court and the ground floor for a time as butchers' shambles. It was demolished in 1850 and replaced by the present Corn Exchange.

59 Another view of Leicester Market Place, by I.C. Cockshaw in 1812. The Exchange stands to the left and the Elizabethan conduit is in the far right (north-east) corner.

60 The Market Place in 1847 with the New Gainsborough exactly 100 years old standing on the site of the later Corn Exchange. Pearce's jeweller's shop can just be made out behind the lamp-post that now surmounts the conduit. This was evidently still in use as a water supply, though the Midland Railway had cut through the water course on Conduit Street from which the supply came.

61 & 62 Two views of Applegate Street in 1892, looking north and south. Applegate, sometimes known as Shambles Lane because of the presence of butchers during the Middle Ages, occupied a site to the west of the present Holiday Inn and was the main road into Leicester for those arriving from the West Bridge. The renaming of a part of High Cross Street with the same name is confusing and regrettable.

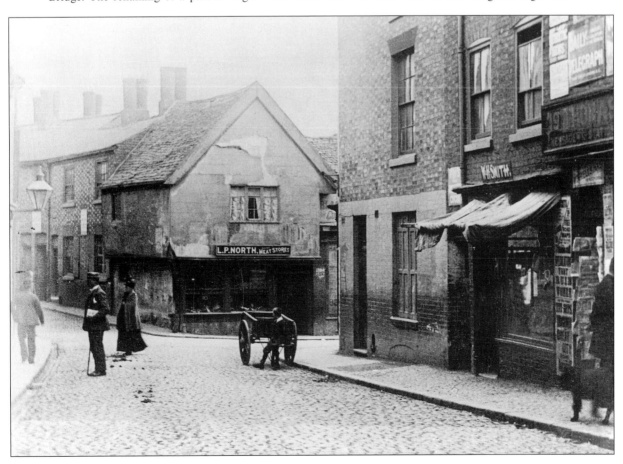

63 William Carey, the Baptist missionary, lived in this house in Thornton Lane when he was pastor at Harvey Lane Chapel, before leaving for his great work in India. Carey's cottage lay in the path of the underpass and was consequently demolished in the late '60s.

64 Mary Linwood (1755-1845) was one of a talented family living at the upper end of Belgrave Gate, where her mother set up a school for young ladies in 1764. Mary created her pictures in worsted wool, producing her first at the age of thirteen. In 1787 she displayed her pictures before the royal family prior to a public exhibition in London.

65 In the early years of the 19th century the town could boast a varied cultural life reflecting the interests and abilities of several leading families. William Gardiner set up a Choral Society that lasted from 1826 to 1841 and he left an intimate portrait of his life and times in *Music and Friends*, published in 1838.

66 An 18th-century view of Stoughton Grange, the site of which is now the Co-op Farm Park, next to Evington golf course. It was the residence of the Powys-Keck family. The extensive estate was sold in 1913 and developed with substantial and elegant housing, much of it now used as University halls of residence. The hall itself was demolished in 1926.

67 A sketch by John Flower of one of the lodges to Stoughton Grange. The lodge still stands on Gartree Road at the entrance to the Farm Park.

68 John Johnson's Assembly Rooms and Hotel of 1792 gave its name to Hotel Street, though it never prospered as a hotel. It was used as judges' lodgings from 1817 and from 1888 was the meeting place of the County Council until it moved into new accommodation at Glenfield. Now called the City Rooms, it remains one of Leicester's most elegant and attractive buildings.

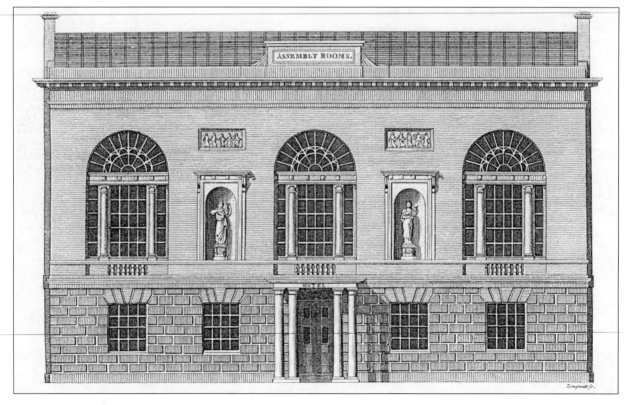

69 The Borough Gaol being demolished in 1880. It was built in 1793 to the design of one Moneypenny, who, according to Susanna Watts, became its first inmate as a debtor. Susanna Watts was the author of one of the earliest town guides, *A Walk Through Leicester*, first published in 1804 and re-printed in 1969.

70 Some mystery surrounds this picture. It is dated 1823 but if this is correct it could not have been in Welford Road prison which was not built till 1828. The date on the picture is almost certainly incorrect. An eye witness, born in 1847, recalled seeing a treadmill as a young girl in Welford Road prison: 'I had once been taken round part of the gaol, and seen a poor man working the tread mill, like a squirrel in a cage. He could not leave off however tired he was—he would have been hit by it. This barbarous machine was done away with long ago.'

71 Until Lloyd George's provision of Old Age Pensions in 1908, the only real social security for the elderly lay in the Poor Laws. This effectively meant that destitute old people were likely to end their days in the workhouse. These were deliberately made grim and unpleasant so that the poor would fear to ask for parish relief and in consequence the poor rates would remain low. In 1836, the Leicester Poor Law Guardians resolved to build their new workhouse where Moat Community College now stands. William Flint's plans met with approval as 'having a neat, homely English appearance, and nothing of the character of a bastille'. The workhouse, later known as Hillcrest Hospital, was demolished in 1977.

72 Archibald Turner's Bow Bridge Works was a splendid early 19th-century hosiery factory designed like a Venetian palace. Its former location is clear from the cupola of Donisthorpe's factory on the far side of the canal seen here above the castellated façade of the Works. They were felled in 1965.

73 The Theatre Royal, designed by William Parsons in 1836, was demolished in 1957. It was perhaps the finest of the half dozen places of theatrical entertainment lost to the town in the middle decades of the 20th century, others being the Opera House, the Empire Theatre, the Temperance Hall, the Palace Theatre, the Floral Hall and the small theatre in the Working Men's Club in Bond Street.

74 There were, confusingly, three houses off London Road known by almost the same name. The first, The Stoney Gate, stood next to Duke's Drive and was probably originally a medieval farmhouse. It was pulled down in about 1955.

75 The second, Stoneygate House, on Toller Road, was built about 1760 by Samuel Oliver, Mayor of Leicester in 1762, and was also demolished about 1955. The site remained empty for over 30 years but has now been absorbed by three substantial houses.

76 The Stonygate of John Biggs was the last to be built, in 1845, and the first to go, in 1862, when his business began to fail. It was demolished to make way for the Victorian villas on Knighton Park Road. Biggs moved for a while to Portland House and then settled in a much humbler terraced house overlooking the Welford Road recreation ground. John Biggs would have thoroughly approved of its being renamed in honour of Nelson Mandela; in 1848, his Stonygate mansion sheltered the Hungarian patriot Louis Kossuth, whom the Queen regarded as a dangerous revolutionary.

77 One of the earliest houses to be built on the Avenue Road estate of the Freehold Land Society. This was owned by Joseph Goddard, the chemist and manufacturer of the famous silver polish. It was demolished in the 1970s to make way for three substantial modern houses on Southernhay Road and a distinguished bungalow on Avenue Road itself, one of the few modern houses to be listed by English Heritage.

78 Wigston Grange is now the headquarters of the Institution of Occupational Safety and Health. It dates from 1823 when it was home to the family of Thomas Burgess, a Quaker woolstapler. In 1846 the Burgesses moved to Brookfield on London Road where Edward Burgess, the architect, was born the following year.

79 Brookfield was built for Thomas Burgess but much altered by Joseph Goddard when it was bought by Thomas Fielding Johnson in 1877. Once the residence of the Bishop of Leicester, it is now the Charles Frear School of Nursing and part of De Montfort University.

80 Leicester's first railway station. The terminus of the Leicester to Swannington line opened in 1832, looking towards West Bridge. The canal flows behind the wooden fence. Another passenger-only platform was built in the 1890s and its opening is advertised in the window of the Goods Office. This view is taken from a lantern slide.

81 Stephenson's Lift Bridge over the canal at Soar Lane. His clever device of his enabled boats to use the canal when the bridge was in the raised position. When lowered, coal trucks could be sent over the canal straight into the yard of Ellis and Everard, the coal merchants.

82 Midland Railway Station in Campbell Street, 1840, demolished in 1892 when the present station was built on London Road.

83 In this photograph of 1856 the outline of Hillcrest Workhouse can be seen in the background rising above the station.

84 The Great Northern and the London and North Western Railway jointly undertook the construction of a new railway in East Leicestershire. Its Leicester terminus, seen here, opened in 1879.

85 Danet's Hall, here illustrated from Throsby's book of 1791, stood to the west of the town near the junction of Fosse Road with King Richard's Road. It belonged to the Danet family from the 15th to the late 17th centuries. In 1700 it came into the hands of John Watts who rebuilt the earlier mansion. He also gave his name to Watts Causeway, later known as King Richard's Road. One of his descendants, Susanna Watts, published the first guide to Leicester in 1804. The last owner, Dr. Noble, one of the town's M.P.s, died while on holiday in Spain in 1861. His estate was purchased by the Leicester Freehold Land Society, a subsidiary of which eventually became the Alliance and Leicester.

86 An early photograph of what is now King Richard's Road looking toward Fosse Road. Taken about 1860, it shows the grounds of Danet's Hall to the right, before the estate was sold to the Freehold Land Society on the death of Dr. Noble.

87 Working-class housing on Dannet Street built in the 1860s. The houses on the left were built with only one main room up and down and were approached by a tunnel through the houses facing onto Dannet Street itself. The density of housing here was four times greater than the owners of the estate, the Leicester Freehold Land Society, intended, but such was the reluctance of central government to limit the sacred rights of free enterprise, that neither the Land Society nor the local council had power to prevent such overcrowding.

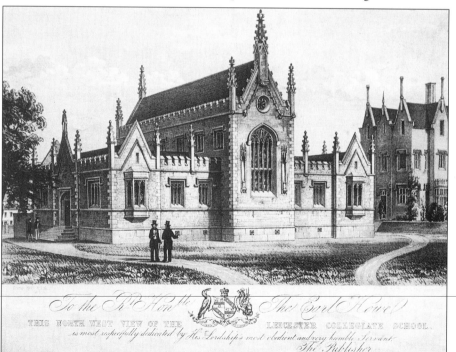

88 By 1836 the Free Grammar School had virtually ceased to function and a new school was projected to meet the needs of wealthier citizens. The governors decided to employ only Anglican masters and, as a result, nonconformists set up a rival institution in New Walk. The Collegiate School, shown here, designed by J. Weightman of Sheffield in a decidedly Gothic style, later became a Congregational chapel and now belongs to the Museums Service.

89 The Museum on New Walk was originally designed by the Roman Catholic Joseph Hansom who also gave his name to the Hansom cab. It was built as The Proprietory School for the sons of the nonconformists who objected to the exclusive Anglicanism of the Collegiate School. It flourished for only ten years and was then purchased as the Town Museum in 1849.

90 Leicestershire and Rutland Lunatic Asylum in 1849. Designed in part by William Parsons in 1835 and extended several times before becoming the University College of Leicester in 1921, it was used as a military hospital during the First World War.

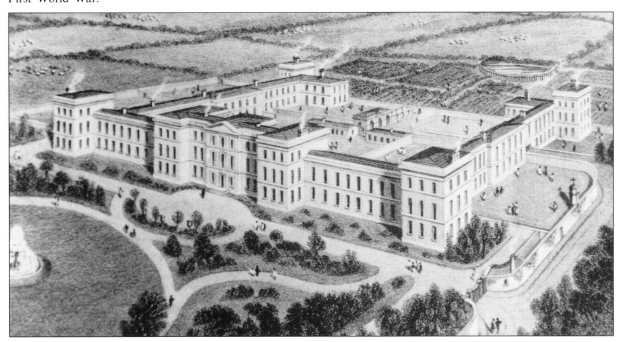

91 Adult Education is one of those needs periodically felt by middle-class benefactors to be necessary for the advancement and improvement of the poor. Invariably, however, such provision tends to cater for the leisure time of the middle classes themselves. The most notable attempt to provide adult education in Victorian Leicester was the Working Men's College in Union Street, established in 1860 by Canon Vaughan.

92 The College building of 1906, by Stockdale Harrison, standing just to the north of St Nicholas' Church, where the underpass is now.

93 Forster's Education Act of 1870 led to the establishment of locally elected School Boards to oversee the elementary education of children where no adequate provision existed. Leicester's School Board opened six schools in 1874 of which this was the first, in King Richard's Road. The architects were Shenton and Baker and the style reflected the Anglican persuasion of Canon Vaughan and the original School Board. From 1876, however, the School Board was controlled by the Liberals and their architect was Edward Burgess. The school is now demolished.

94 Built on the site of a private swimming bath opposite Holy Cross Priory on New Walk, this was a Roman Catholic school. In later years it became a Sikh temple. Charnwood Court now stands in its place.

95 The Wyggeston Girls School junior department, in the garden of 17 Friar Lane, known as Dr. Benfield's house in about 1908. The girls are wearing their straw 'benjies' and playing one-stump cricket. The spire of St Martin's and the main block of Alderman Newton's School are in the background.

96 & 97   The General News Room 1838, designed by William Flint, incorporated a Library and Reading Room. The annual subscription of one guinea was enough to deter working-class membership. However, Leicester had to wait till 1869 for the opening of its first free library, when the Mechanics' Institute relinquished its tenure of the New Hall and handed over its stock of books to the new public library. The News Room was demolished in 1898 and replaced by the present building, built in a similar style by Joseph Goddard.

98 The *Three Crowns Hotel*, said to have been built in 1726, was demolished in 1867 to make room for the new National Provincial Bank. This was Leicester's main coaching inn and the last stage coach is seen here leaving in 1866.

99 The Corn Exchange was built in two stages: the ground floor by William Flint in 1850, the upper floor and 'Rialto Bridge' by another architect, F.W. Ordish, five years later. There had been an earlier building on this spot, known as 'The Gainsborough', since the Middle Ages. It was used for various purposes, including a gaol, a magistrates' court and assembly rooms. Here we see the building of 1851 prior to the additions by Ordish.

100 Evington village at the turn of the century. The thatched cottage stands where Errington's garage is now. The pretty Gothic chapel on the corner of High Street was originally built for the Countess of Huntingdon's Connexion, a sort of Methodist mission to the middle classes promoted by the Countess Selina in the late 18th century. The chapel is now used by the Particular Baptists.

101 St George's Church, designed by William Parsons, was the first to be built in 19th-century Leicester. It was carved out of the sprawling parish of St Margaret's to minister to the spiritual needs of the suburban population to the south of the town. It lost its spire during a disastrous fire in 1911 and was entirely rebuilt at that time.

102 Welford Road Cemetery was originally proposed as a nonconformist venture, denominational differences being too strong at the time to contemplate fraternisation even in death. Good sense prevailed, however, and the grounds were laid out to cater for all faiths, opening in 1849. The chapels seen here were sadly demolished in the 1960s.

103 Leicester Cathedral. The medieval church of St Martin, situated next to the old Town Hall, always played an important part in the civic life of the town. Charles I twice attended services here and in 1921 it was chosen as the cathedral church of the new diocese of Leicester. Restored several times in the Victorian period, its tower and spire were added in 1862 rising to 220 feet.

104 The interior of St Mark's Church, Belgrave, the masterpiece of the architect Ewan Christian. It was paid for by the Perry-Herricks of Beaumanor to provide for the working-class district to the north of the town. Its second incumbent, Canon Donaldson, achieved some notoriety as a champion of the poor by leading the first march of unemployed men to London in 1905. He was also responsible for the painting of the seven great murals in the apse, depicting the Travail and Triumph of Labour.

105 Emanuel Baptist Church used to stand out above the terraced housing to the west of the town. Designed by Shenton and Baker in 1871, it stood for just over 100 hundred years and was demolished to allow for the extension of Narborough Road to King Richard's Road.

106 Melbourne Hall, built to accommodate the preaching talents of the Rev. F.B. Meyer, who later became President of the Free Church Federal Council in London. It was designed by Joseph Goddard in 1880 and even today it dominates the Leicester skyline.

107 The Secular Hall in Humberstone Gate was opened in 1881 to provide a meeting place for Leicester's outspoken rationalists. William Morris spoke here, as did Charles Bradlaugh, Annie Besant and George Bernard Shaw. The façade was embellished with the busts of five great figures in the development of human thought, including Jesus. This gesture of respect to the Christian community backfired, led by Canon Vaughan, who objected to Christ being placed alongside such infidels as Tom Paine, Voltaire and Robert Owen.

108-110 One essential feature of a thriving commercial town is the provision of an adequate post office. The need for new premises in Leicester concerned contemporaries almost as much as the need for a new town hall. There were three built here on the same site in Granby Street. The first, in elegant classical style, was demolished and replaced by the rather ponderous and functional Italianate building of 1867. As the town grew so did its postal needs, and the Victorian office of 1885 was built, echoing the French Gothic of Goddard's Midland Bank in the background. It survived till 1930s when the present post office was built in neighbouring Bishop Street.

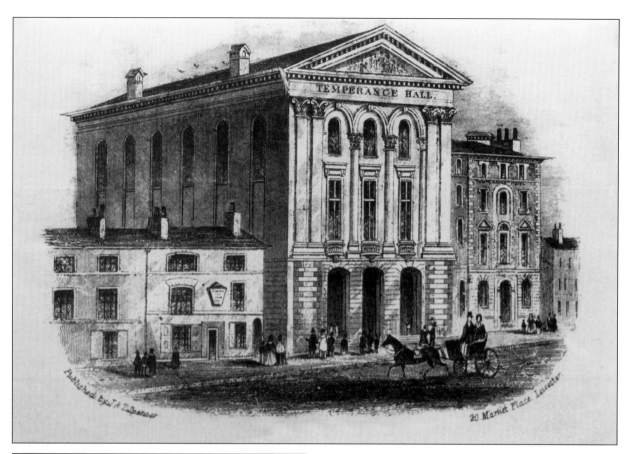

111 Black's Camping shop in Granby Street began life in 1853 as the *Commercial Hotel* run by Marianne Cook for the benefit of her husband's teetotal visitors to Leicester. The entrance to the hotel yard is next to the shop. The Temperance Hall used to stand on the left of this. Both were designed by the architect, James Medland.

112 John Meadows' Midland Distillery, designed by J.F. Smith in 1869, on the corner of Clarence Street and Humberstone Gate. It has a fine pannelled smoking room above the front entrance where potential customers were entertained. Given its origin, it seems quite appropriate that it should have become a wine bar.

113 The building in the centre of this photograph incorporated the old Assembly Rooms. It was demolished in 1868 and the Clock Tower erected on the site. The view is taken from High Street, with New Bond Street on the left and Cheapside to the right.

114 A late Victorian view of the Clock Tower, designed by Joseph Goddard and erected in 1868. John Burton, the photographer, had been instrumental in arranging the competition to erect a monument here in front of his premises. As secretary to the East Gates Improvement Committee, he had a hard job persuading the council to spend ratepayers' money, and a public subscription was raised to pay for the Clock Tower. To illustrate the degree of congestion in the area, Leicester's first traffic census was held here in 1861. It recorded 54,300 pedestrians, 2,960 vehicles, 5,900 drivers and passengers apart, from numerous animals.

Commemorated on the Clock Tower are four benefactors of the town: Simon de Montfort, William Wyggeston, Thomas White, who left money for the encouragement of new businesses, and Alderman Newton, who founded a charity school in 1753.

115 The Town Hall of Leicester, designed by J.F. Hames, 1872. It is the first municipal building in the 'Queen Anne' style. The council was reluctant to spend money on a grandiose public hall as there were several then standing, such as Thomas Cook's Temperance Hall. Consequently the term Town Hall is a misnomer, there being no public place of assembly in the building. Nevertheless, the council decided in March 1876 that the new buildings then nearing completion should henceforth be known as 'The Town Hall of the Borough of Leicester'.

116 An airman's view of Leicester in the early '20s. The Town Hall is as yet without its rear extension and the Theatre Royal faces Horsefair Street. The back of John Johnson's hotel, now the City Rooms, can be seen behind, while, in the top right corner, the white gables of Pearce's the Jeweller's in the Market Place can be seen below the classical frontage of the Co-operative Bank and the more grandiose National Westminster Bank on St Martins.

117 Granby Street outside the *Grand Hotel*, with an assortment of horse-drawn carts and electric trams. The old post office can be seen on the left opposite the pinnacled splendour of the Victoria Coffee House.

118 The Victoria Coffee House opened in 1888. It was the most palatial and opulent of the dozen establishments run by the Leicester Coffee and Cocoa House Company in an effort to wean the workers away from alcoholic drink. This advertisement appeared in a directory of 1890. By 1908, The Victoria had been sold to Sir Herbert Marshall as new premises for his music store. The Coffee and Cocoa House Company as a whole ceased trading in 1922.

119 A rather wet view of the new entrance to the Market Place in 1902. Prior to the creation of this opening, a continuous line of shops stood here, in place of the old town wall and the nearest entry to the market was via East Gate. On the left is Inglesant's 'Atlas' Furniture Store (note the figure of Atlas on the roof). The trams, still horse-drawn, are seen against the murky outline of the Town Hall, while to the right, in the Market Place, the Corn Exchange is not yet obscured by permanent market stalls.

"THE VICTORIA" COFFEE HOUSE,

GRANBY STREET, LEICESTER, OPPOSITE THE GENERAL POST OFFICE.

(Opened December 20, 1888, by her Grace the DUCHESS OF RUTLAND.)

THE LEICESTER
COFFEE AND COCOA HOUSE
COMPANY, LIMITED.

List of Houses, open from 5 a.m. to 11 p.m.

1.—"THE GRANBY."
5, GRANBY STREET, near General P.O.

2.—"THE RUTLAND."
Corner of WHARF STREET and HUMBERSTONE ROAD.

3.—"THE HIGHCROSS."
Corner of HIGH STREET and HIGHCROSS STREET.

4.—"THE MIDLAND."
CAMPBELL ST., near Railway Station.

5.—"THE EASTGATES"
Near the CLOCK TOWER.

6.—"THE WELFORD."
Corner of MARLBOROUGH STREET and WELFORD ROAD.

7.—"THE ALBERT."
BELGRAVE GATE, Corner of New Parliament Street.

8.—"THE WEST BRIDGE."
Near the WEST BRIDGE.

9.—"THE GREAT NORTHERN."
Opposite the GREAT NORTHERN RAILWAY STATION, BELGRAVE ROAD.

10.—"THE COBDEN."
Corner of HUMBERSTONE ROAD and COBDEN STREET.

11.—"THE ST. MARGARET'S."
Corner of LOWER CHURCH GATE, near St. Margaret's Church.

12.—"THE VICTORIA."
GRANBY STREET, opposite the General Post Office.

13.—"THE PAVILION."
VICTORIA PARK, open during the Summer months.

General Price List.

Cup of Coffee	Cheese Cake .... } 1d.
French Coffee, small cup	Twist ....
Cup of Chocolate..	Pork Pie ......
Cup of Tea	Sausage Roll....
Superior Tea, small cup ..... } 1d.	Ham Sandwich ... } 2d.
Glass of Milk	College Pudding
Plate of Potatoes..	Plate of Ham ...
Hot Sausages	Plate of Corned Beef......2d. and 1d.
Roll and Butter ..	Corn Beef Sandwich .... } 1½d.
Roll and Cheese ..	Bun ....
Lunch Cake	Roll .... } ½d.
Custard	Biscuit ....
Scotch Scone......	

Soda and Milk, per glass, 1½d. and 2d.

Lemonade Splits,
Soda Water Splits,
Ginger Ale,
Ginger Beer, } 1d. per bottle.

Lime Juice, per glass, 1d.

Soup from 11 until 2—Per basin, 2d.; half-basin, 1d.

Cigars, 3d. each; 2d. each, or 7 for 1s.; 1½d. each, or 9 for 1s.

Tea, Coffee and Cocoa sold out-door, at reduced rates.

FIRST-CLASS REFRESHMENT ROOMS,
(1ST FLOOR,)

"VICTORIA," Open from 8 a.m. till 10-30 p.m.
"EASTGATES," Open from 10 a.m. till 10-30 p.m.

Price List.

Cup of Coffee ..	Fruit Pies, hot or cold, 2d.
Cup of Chocolate } 1½d.	Soda and Milk, per Glass......2d. and 3d.
Cup of Tea......	Glass of Milk ....
Bun	Hot Sausages ....
Roll .... } 1d.	Roll and Butter ..
Biscuits	Roll and Cheese ..
Pork Pie........	Lunch Cake...... } 1½d.
Sausage Roll....	Custard ....
Ham Sandwich..	Scotch Scone ....
Beef ditto	Cheese Cake ....
Plate of Ham .. } 3d.	Twist...........
Plate of Corned Beef	Ginger Beer.. } 1½d. and
Pudding	Ginger Ale .. } 2d. per bot.
Potatoes .... } 2d	Lemonade.......
Boiled Egg......	Soda Water ..... } 1½d.
	Lime Juice, per gl.

Dinners Daily (see Bill of Fare).
Steaks and Chops on the shortest notice.
Hot Joints from 12 to 2—Per plate, 7d.
Soup from 11 until 2—Per plate, 3d.

JAS. JOHNSON, Secretary, 4, Millstone Lane.
H. HARVEY, General Manager, The Stores, Marlborough Street.

120 A view of the grandstand on Victoria Park. The race course was removed from its London Road site in 1883 when the new race course at Oadby came into being. The remaining space became known, at first derisively, as Victoria Park; it had none of the hallmarks of a true public park such as the ornamental flower beds, lakes, grotto and bandstand that featured prominently in the newly created Abbey Park, opened in 1882.

121 When the Corporation first decided to erect public swimming baths in 1876 in Bath Lane, their plans were attacked as wasteful. The government in London saw no need to provide swimming baths for women. The project, reduced in scale and expense, was built to the design of J.B. Everard, nephew of the brewer, and opened in 1879. Some remember them affectionately for their 'green water and black beetles'. This photo was taken shortly before their demolition in the late 1960s.

122 The lime kilns shown here gave their name to Lime Kiln Lock, next to Abbey Park and Charles Keene College of Further Education. In the background is the spire of St Mark's Church and, on the right, the original Gas Works.

123 The old gas works off Belgrave Road. The first meeting of the private Gas Company was held in the *Saracen's Head* in 1821. It was bought out by the Corporation in 1877 at the same time as it acquired the waterworks. In the top left corner of this photograph can be seen the present Library block of Charles Keene College, and in the foreground, beside the canal, is the Friday Street depot of the council's sanitary department. To the right, the trees are in front of Corah's St Margaret's Works and Burley's Way does not yet exist.

124 Gas Museum, Aylestone Road, by the architects, Shenton and Baker. The clock tower and row of workers' cottages date from 1879 when the gas works was purchased by the Corporation and moved to this site from its earlier location by the canal wharf on Belgrave Road.

125 The rather unusual hoop of red brick that greets visitors to Leicester as they pass over West Bridge is a remnant of the old wholesale vegetable and fish market that formerly stood in Rutland Street. It incorporates the sculpture of mermaids and fishes by Walter Brand, seen here over the entrance to the old market.

126 & 127 This tile decoration on High Street shows Thomas Butler, a chemist noted for his patent medicine 'Seabreeze', for which the advertisement shown here makes considerable claims. Victorian chemists filled much the same role as health clinics today, providing remedies for most ills without entailing the expense of attendance by doctors. Like Butler, they were anxious to assure customers of their professional qualifications.

TAKE COUNSEL

& see that you get —

BUTLERS.

A CHAT ABOUT INFLUENZA

During recent years influenza has become quite a scourge in European countries, and even in England outbreaks are almost an annual occurrence. Year after year it claims its thousands of victims, while many who recover from its first results feel its evil after-effects for years. The first symptoms are dizziness, pains in the head, back and throat, general languor, increase of temperature, sometimes accompanied by sudden chill and shivering. If you feel any of these symptons keep in a warm room and adopt a light diet. To cut short the attack send for a packet of

Butlers' Influenza Powders,

which are highly recommended as a safe and speedy antidote. They are equally valuable in cases of common colds and fevers.

Sold in Packets 1/3, or 3 for 2d.
SEND NOW. Have them Handy.

T. E. BUTLER, SON & Co.

Sole Proprietors,

Seabreeze Factory, CARTS LANE, Leicester.

Sold by all Patent Medicine Dealers.

128 Much of Leicester's prosperity in the later 19th century grew out of the expansion of ancillary trades such as the manufacture of laces for the shoe industry. The most prominent of the firms supplying these was Faire Brothers, with their superb warehouse, Alexandra House, designed by Edward Burgess on the corner of Queen Street and Southampton Street. Nikolaus Pevsner calls it 'palatial ... and one of the finest in the country'. The terracotta detailing and mosaic entrance are still exquisite, but the copper dome was destroyed during the Second World War.

129 The humble boot-lace answers a universal need, as this charming advertisement implies. It suggests the quality and strength of the Faire Brothers' product but reminds one also of some more modern, deliberately pretentious advertisements for products such as milk chocolate. Was this the lace that launched a thousand ships?

WINN'S ORIENTAL CAFÉ.

NATIONAL TELEPHONE 608.

COLD LUNCHEONS, SOUPS, TEAS, &c., &c.

HANDSOME AND SPACIOUS TEA ROOMS, GROUND FLOOR

All the BAMBOO FITTINGS in the Café were Manufactured on the Premises.

ESTIMATES submitted for Specialities and Oriental Decorations in Japanese style.

COMFORTABLE AND COMMODIOUS SMOKE ROOMS, FIRST FLOOR.

SPÉCIALITÉ.—CUP OF DELICIOUS COFFEE WITH CREAM, AND CIGARETTE, 2d.

New Billiard and Chess Club Rooms. Two splendid new Tables fitted with the patent pneumatic cushions. Open 10 a.m. to 10.30 p.m.

J. S. WINN & CO.,

Tea and Coffee Specialists, Manufacturers of Bamboo Art Furniture, Importers of Japanese and Oriental Novelties,

18, MARKET PLACE, LEICESTER.

---

130 Retailing sometimes combined with the manufacture of specialist goods. Winn encouraged customers at his Oriental Café to sit at tables and chairs made on the premises in the Market Place. Winn's tea rooms exuded an air of oriental extravagance and mystery. Note the supply of free cigarettes with a coffee and cream!

131 Among the many firms originating in Leicester which later became household names was the umbrella factory of William Kendall. His hair-dressing business led him to offer his clients protection from the English weather, and, by 1884, newspaper advertisements boasted of his Northampton Street factory:

> They're made there for his retail trade,
> With light substantial frames,
> And choicest sticks and fabrics rich,
> For gentlemen or dames.

132 Tyler's shoe warehouse in Rutland Street, on the corner of Colton Street, built in 1875. The Tylers evidently found Italianate architecture to their liking as their house in Humberstone Park adopted a similar style, not often found in Leicester.

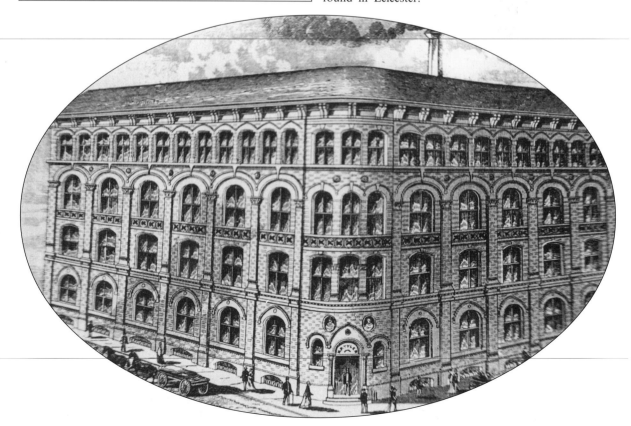

133 Nathaniel Corah set up as a hosier in 1815. His sons and grandsons enlarged the business and Corah's St Margaret's Works opened in 1865, quickly establishing its hold on the hosiery trade by utilising steam-powered rotary machines. From 1926 the firm supplied Marks and Spencer with their St Michael and St Margaret brands.

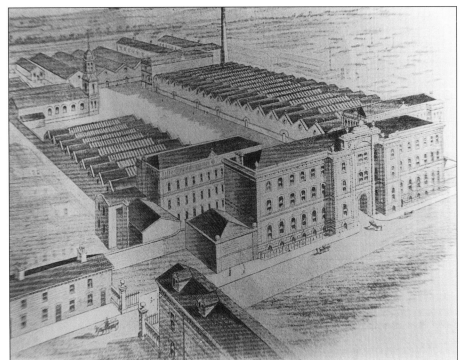

134 Several makers of cycles operated from Leicester, including Parr's of Belgrave Gate. More long-lasting and well-known was the business started by William Curry in Painter Street, off Belgrave Road, in the 1880s.

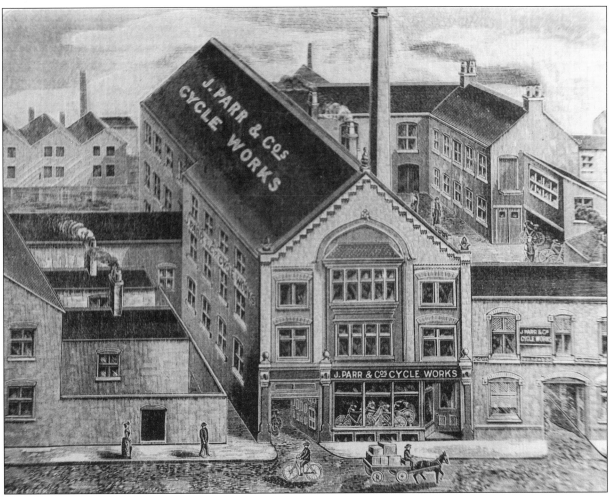

135 Belgrave Gate in the 1890s. The Palace Theatre can be seen on the left and the spire of St Mark's in the distance.

136 Bedford Square in Belgrave Gate at the junction with Bedford Street.

137 The Palace Theatre, Belgrave Gate, shortly before its demolition in the 1960s.

138 A water-colour sketch of the Castle and St Mary de Castro seen from the river bank before the flood-prevention works and canalisation of the Soar in 1890. This is probably the work of John Flower's daughter, Elizabeth.

139 Work in progress for the deepening and widening of the canal and prevention of flooding, south of the West Bridge, in 1890. St Mary de Castro spire can be made out in the background.

140 Before the deepening and widening of the canal, the land south of the West Bridge was a flood plain, notable for its withy or osier beds for making baskets. The area was partly used for allotments and remained rather untidy until the creation of Castle Gardens in 1926.

141 The De Montfort Hall, designed by Shirley Harrison in 1912. It is seen here in the 1930s with the fire station of 1927 and the Wyggeston Girls School, 1928, in the background. The open-air theatre can be seen in the gardens to the left.

142 Granby Street decked out for the Coronation of George V. Brass-helmeted firemen on horse-drawn pumps pass Thomas Cook's Temperance Hall. The corner of the Y.M.C.A. is on the far left.

143 A delightful photograph, taken in 1912, of two young children with their nurse-maids and their mother, with her bicycle, in Shady Lane, Evington.

144 St Peter's Church and Highfield Street, 1911. St Peter's, designed by G.E. Street, lost its broach spire in the 1960s. An open-topped electric tram can be seen on the single track at St Peter's Road.

145 Evington Street, Highfields. Much of the Victorian town was swept away in re-development during the 1960s, though some of what replaced it lasted nothing like as long as what was then deemed unfit. Whole streets of working-class housing vanished without even a pictorial record. Fortunately one man did his best to record what was there. Dennis Calow has a vast collection of photographs, of which this is an example.

146 Evington Street in the course of demolition, 1965. The church in the background is now the Polish Roman Catholic Church in Melbourne Road.

147 Prior to the establishment of the Local Board of Health in 1849, there was virtually no control over house-building. These cottages that stood next to St George's churchyard, opposite the present *Leicester Mercury* building, probably date from the 1820s. They had one room up and one downstairs, with a communal tap and one privy between three. Note the round chimneys and gas lamp.

148 Some of the working-class housing off Burley's Way about to be demolished, in the 1930s. The inhabitants moved to the new council estates that ringed Leicester.

149 Early Victorian housing at the lower end of New Walk, demolished in the early '60s after a prolonged attack of 'planners' blight'. They were replaced by a graceless concrete office block on one side and a slightly more acceptable pastiche on the other.

150 Houses on East Street shortly before demolition in the late 1950s. The Y.M.C.A. is on the right and the spire still crowning St John's Church can be seen in the background.

151 Houses on Welford Road, opposite the prison, which were demolished in 1966. The tenants of the upper floors used to command high prices for their grandstand view of public executions.

152 An early 19th-century terrace on Welford Road, opposite Tower Street, typical of the modest but gracious buildings so carelessly sacrificed by the developers in the 1960s.

153 The Abbey Pumping Station. Leicester's first modern network of sewers, laid down in the 1850s, discharged into the works of the Patent Solid Sewerage Manufacturing Company to the north of the Abbey lands. As the town expanded, the plant became overloaded and an entirely new system, based on sewage irrigation of farm land at Beaumont Leys, was adopted. This necessitated sending the sewage in pipes up 65 feet from the pumping station seen here.

154 & 155 From 1890 sewage was pumped from the Abbey Pumping Station to the fields around Beaumont Leys farm. Here men can be seen hoeing beans and sorting eggs on the sewage farm in the 1930s. The scheme became redundant in 1965 with the opening of the works at Wanlip.

156-158 Three vehicles belonging to the Tramways and Omnibus Department. Horse-drawn trams ran in Leicester from 1872 and were electrified in 1904 soon after the Corporation purchased the undertaking. Petrol-driven buses rapidly established their advantage in flexibility, especially in outlying districts. The new garage opened on Abbey Park Road in 1926, a year before these photographs were taken.

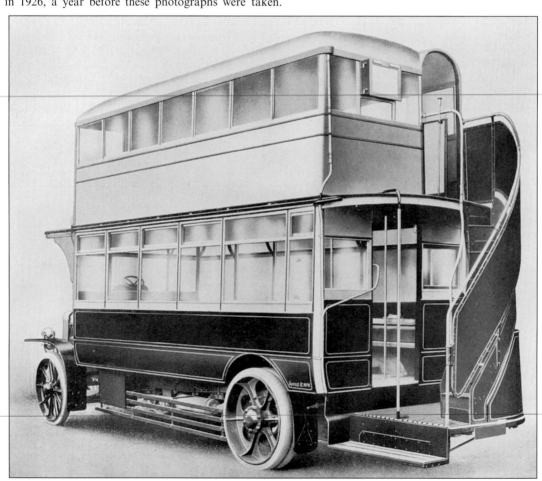

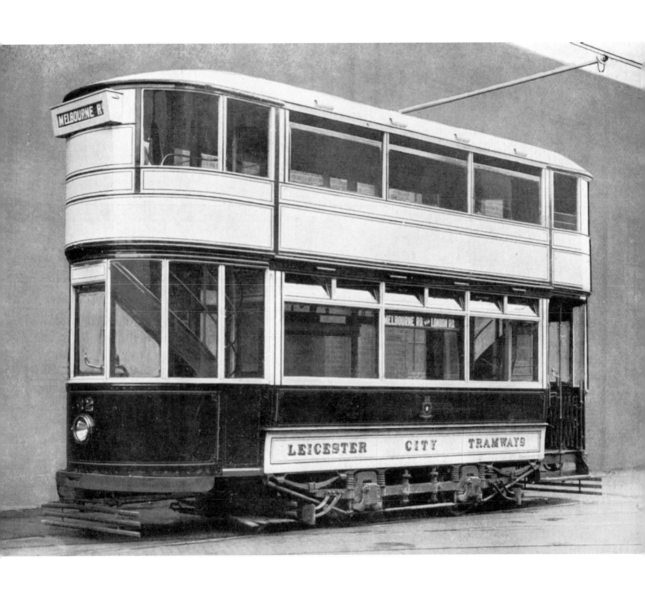

159 The new railway bridge over Aylestone Road being lowered into position on the Burton line of the Midland Railway in May 1932.

160 A locomotive at Saffron Lane crossing on the branch line to Burton-on-Trent in 1928, before the building of the bridge.

161 A steam train on the Great Central line seen here from the top of Mowacre Hill.

162 Narborough Road in 1926, looking towards the town. The motor car was still a rare sight and gas lamps still provided street lighting. The farm on the left, New Fields Farm, was just outside the borough boundary. It used to sell fresh country produce to the public. The farmhouse was demolished in 1929.

163 Sheep being driven down Saffron Lane, after the blizzard of 31 March 1916, at the Aylestone and Wigston crossroads, where the notorious roundabout on the A563 stands today.

164 & 165 Lloyd George's promise of 'homes fit for heroes to live in' bore fruit in the Addison Act of 1919. Leicester was one of the first local authorities to erect council houses under this Act. A campaign in favour of concrete as the modern construction material led the council to award contracts to the Sheffield firm of Henry Boot and Company. In fact the houses proved more expensive than brick-built ones and long-term structural problems have led to their demolition and replacement.

The Park Housing Estate was still being developed in 1927, when it was surrounded by farmland. The semi-circular shape of Elston recreation ground is in the centre, while to the top left the railway severs any connection with the fields of West Knighton.

The Bell Hotel and Humberstone Gate, Leicester

166 The *Bell Hotel* in Humberstone Gate, an 18th-century coaching inn which served as the meeting place for the directors of the Leicester-Swannington Railway among its many other functions. It was lost in the wholesale redevelopment of the Haymarket in the 1960s.

167 Charles Street in the 1950s. The spire of St Peter's church rising above the Police Station.

168 Queens Building of De Montfort University is a rhapsodic celebration of post-modernism, far removed from the impersonal concrete slab constructions of the third quarter of the 20th century. It has much more than its looks to recommend it, being one of the most energy-efficient structures to be built in Britain.

169 This arresting view of a steam train on the old Great Central line was taken through an arch of the Jewry Wall before the construction of the present Vaughan College. The semi-circular shape of a cold plunge bath can be seen at the western end of the Roman baths. The photograph, from Colin Walker's *Main Line Lament* (1973), brings together such diverse elements of the past that it seems a fitting image with which to conclude this pictorial record of Leicester's history.

Index

Roman numerals refer to pages in the introduction, and arabic numerals to individual illustrations.